American Impressionism
Paintings of Light and Life

Fig. 2. William Chadwick (1879–1962). **IRISES**, n.d. Oil on canvas, 25 x 30 in.
Florence Griswold Museum, Gift of Elizabeth Chadwick O'Connell, 1975.7.5

American Impressionism Paintings of Light and Life

BY MEGAN HOLLOWAY FORT, PH.D.
AND DIANE E. FORSBERG

*Featuring 12 Paintings
from the Arkell Museum
at Canajoharie, and the Arkell
Hall Foundation Collections*
www.arkellmuseum.org

Fenimore Art Museum, Cooperstown, New York
www.fenimoreartmuseum.org

American Impressionism Paintings of Light and Life

BY MEGAN HOLLOWAY FORT, PH.D.
AND DIANE E. FORSBERG

Editor: PAUL S. D'AMBROSIO, PH.D.
Design: RICHARD P. NADEAU

First published in 2012 by the Fenimore Art Museum
Lake Road – P.O. Box 800, Cooperstown, NY 13326
www.fenimoreartmuseum.org

Published in conjunction with the exhibition
American Impressionism: Paintings of Light and Life,
on view at the Fenimore Art Museum, Cooperstown, NY,
May 26–September 16, 2012.

Production: Nadeau Design Associates, Utica, NY
Printing: Monroe Litho, Rochester, NY
Exhibition Management and Design: Michelle Murdock,
Christine Rossi, Stephen Loughman, and Christine Olsen

Cover: Willard Leroy Metcalf (1858–1925). CHILD IN
SUNLIGHT, 1915. Oil on canvas, 25⅛ x 21 in. *Florence
Griswold Museum, Gift of Mrs. Henriette Metcalf, 1979.7.3*

Opposite: Fig. 3. Childe Hassam (1859–1935)
AT THE QUAI, PONT AVEN, 1897. Oil on canvas, 18⅜ x 21⅞ in.
Arkell Hall Foundation

Contents: Fig. 4. William Merritt Chase (1849–1916)
THE CONNOISSEUR-IN THE STUDIO CORNER, ca. 1885
Oil on canvas, 20⅛ x 24⅛ in. *Arkell Museum at Canajoharie,
Gift of Bartlett Arkell, 1945*

Exhibition Sponsors: Fenimore Asset Management, Golden Artist
Colors, and the Beryl P. Haas Charitable Remainder Unitrust

ISBN: 978-0-917334-42-9

Contents

Foreword

PAUL S. D'AMBROSIO, PH.D.
President and CEO

OUR EXHIBITION AND CATALOG *American Impressionism: Paintings of Light and Life* celebrates the sheer visual joy of exploring the effects of light on the variegated world around us. This revolutionary style of painting, imported from France in the 1880s, became a staple of American art by the turn of the century. The works of art in this exhibition represent the output of many of the significant artists who embraced this style and adapted its precepts to the American scene.

In undertaking this project we were fortunate to have the expertise of Megan Holloway Fort, a scholar with a great deal of experience in American Impressionism. Megan thoughtfully guided us in our pursuit of loans and authored the lead essay and expanded captions in this volume. For her enthusiasm for the subject and skill in bringing out the unique qualities of these artworks, we are most grateful.

This exhibition would not have been possible were it not for the cooperation of the Arkell Museum at Canajoharie, New York. We have long known of the Arkell's remarkable collection of American art, and have always had in the back of our minds the possibility of collaboration. American Impressionism presented an ideal opportunity, as the works in this style collected by Bartlett Arkell for the museum are of such high quality and importance that they provided a stunning core of artworks around which we could build the exhibition.

We are, therefore, deeply grateful to the board and staff of the Arkell Museum, particularly Deputy Director and Chief Curator Diane Forsberg, for the enthusiastic response to our initial inquiries about partnering on this project. Diane is the ideal colleague; highly knowledgeable and very committed to sharing her scholarship. Her essay herein on Bartlett Arkell and the American Impressionists brings new scholarship to the field and the public.

A number of other lenders generously made their collections available. Of particular note is the Florence Griswold Museum, located in one of the prime areas for plein-air Impressionist painting. The Griswold's collection is exceptional; their loans have allowed us to provide insights into the making of these artworks, as well as their enduring sense of place. For that we are most grateful to Director Jeff Andersen and his staff.

This lovely catalog is once again the handiwork of Nadeau Design Associates, and their knack for adapting our content to the printed page is startlingly evident. Lastly, as always, the highly skilled staff at the Fenimore Art Museum has taken this material and created a dynamic and meaningful experience for our public. In recent years we have become known for our American art exhibitions, and that is a tribute to the hard work and dedication they consistently bring to our galleries.

Fig. 5
Theodore Robinson (1852–1896)
JOSEPHINE IN THE GARDEN (AT THE FOUNTAIN), ca. 1890
Oil on canvas, 32 ¼ x 26 ⅛ in.
Arkell Museum at Canajoharie, Gift of Bartlett Arkell, 1946

Optimism, Nostalgia and Tradition
Impressionism in the United States

BY MEGAN HOLLOWAY FORT, PH.D.

THE STORY OF American Impressionism begins in 1886, when the Paris-based art dealer Paul Durand-Ruel organized an exhibition of French Impressionist paintings in New York. Comprising nearly three hundred paintings by Edgar Degas, Edouard Manet, Claude Monet, Berthe Morisot, Camille Pissarro, Pierre-Auguste Renoir, and Alfred Sisley, the *Special Exhibition of Works in Oil and Pastel by The Impressionists of Paris* opened at the American Art Association on April 10.[1] Despite the controversy stirred in the press by the avant-garde quality of the works on view, the show was so popular that it was transferred to the National Academy of Design, where it opened on May 25 with additional loans from a small group of New York collections and works by Mary Cassatt. Durand-Ruel is reported to have earned some $40,000 from the exhibition, which marked the beginning of serious interest in Impressionist art on behalf not only of American collectors, but also American painters.

Indeed, the 1886 exhibition acted as a powerful catalyst for American artists, especially those who would come to be known as The Ten—Childe Hassam, John H. Twachtman, Julian Alden Weir, Frank Weston Benson, Joseph Rodefer De Camp, Thomas Dewing, Willard Metcalf, Robert Reid, Edward E. Simmons, Edmund C. Tarbell, and later William Merritt Chase. Almost immediately following the show, and throughout the next decade, nearly all of them underwent significant changes in their work. In general, these artists shifted from an academic style that was controlled, deliberate, crafted in the studio, and marked by an absolute precision of finish, to embrace the expressive brushwork, unfinished paint surface, light high-keyed palette, informal compositions, and plein-air technique that are the hallmarks of Impressionist painting.

But while the American Impressionists embraced the style of the French movement, they shied away from their subject matter. The shopgirls, courtesans, and performers who inhabited the city scenes of Manet and Degas (fig. 7), for example, were replaced by young mothers and elegant women in the canvases of Hassam, Benson, Tarbell, and Chase. Suburban retreats, another favorite subject of both the French and American Impressionists, were also treated completely differently by each group. Monet's views of Argenteuil (fig. 8), for example, often feature railroads, smokestacks, and other evidence of the troublesome conjunction of urban and rural life. For painters on this side of the Atlantic, small country towns were symbols of an unchanging, religious, and patriotic America.

A closer look at the exceptional group of works the Fenimore Art Museum has brought together for this exhibition illustrates that while

Above: Fig. 7
Edgar Degas (1834–1917)
IN A CAFÉ, ALSO CALLED ABSINTHE (ELLEN ANDRÉE AND MARCELLIN DESBOUTIN), 1875–76
Oil on canvas, 36 7/32 x 26 31/32 in.
Musée d'Orsay, Paris, France.
© Réunion des Musées Nationaux/
Art Resources, NY.
Photo: Hervé Lewandowski
Not in exhibition

Opposite: Fig. 6
John Twachtman (1853–1902)
GLOUCESTER HARBOR, ca. 1900
Oil on canvas, 25 x 25 in.
Arkell Museum at Canajoharie,
Gift of Bartlett Arkell, 1939

the American Impressionists adopted an avant-garde style that had been born in opposition to the traditions and conventions of the academy, they often used those aesthetic principles to paint works that were traditional and conventional. The choices they made in terms of what to paint, and how to paint it, reflect the special conditions of American life in the 1890s, a period characterized by a huge wave of immigrants creating new tensions between social classes and ethnic groups, labor unrest and strikes, an economic depression that lasted from 1873 to 1896, and surges in patriotism that resulted from military conflicts such as the Spanish-American War of 1898, the Boxer Rebellion in China in 1900, and the First World War of 1914 to 1918. The choice on behalf of artists to depict subjects that maintained a sense of a unified, harmoniously ordered world were deeply rooted in the conditions and ideology of American life in this period.

William Merritt Chase was the first American painter to successfully incorporate Impressionist values and techniques into his art. Although he had met Cassatt and seen Impressionist work in Paris in 1881, and had begun to paint outdoors in Holland in 1884, it was only in New York in 1886, about the time of the Durand-Ruel exhibition, that he became fully committed to plein-air painting in the Impressionist mode. Roaming the city with portable equipment he had designed, and painting on the spot, he preferred not to use an umbrella, he said, because "I want all the light I can get."[2] The series of small paintings of parks and harbors in Brooklyn and New York City he created between 1886 and 1890, among them *Bath Beach: A Sketch (Bensonhurst)* (fig. 9), are recognized today as the earliest

Fig. 8
Claude Monet (1840–1926)
THE BASIN OF ARGENTEUIL, ca. 1872
Oil on canvas, 23 ^{10}/$_{16}$ x 31 ^{11}/$_{16}$ in.
Musée d'Orsay, Paris, France.
© Réunion des Musées Nationaux/Art Resources, NY.
Photograph by Hervé Lewandowski
Not in exhibition

significant American landscape paintings in the Impressionist style.[3] The works marked a clear departure from the artist's practice of inventing scenes in his studio, though works such as *The Connoisseur-In the Studio Corner* (fig. 4) of about 1881 exhibit characteristics—lively brushwork, vitality, immediacy—that anticipate his Impressionist style.

Bath Beach: A Sketch (Bensonhurst) depicts the seaside walkway along Bensonhurst Drive in the suburban Brooklyn resort of Bath Beach, a quiet, rural spot ideal for families wishing to escape the oppressive heat of the city.[4] In the 1880s, the road was lined by stylish hotels and yacht clubs, while farther inland stood summer villas occupied mainly by middle- and upper-class women and children whose husbands and fathers joined them there on weekends. Thus for a contemporary audience, Chase's painting would have reflected the respectability of the resort, where women and children could stroll carelessly while enjoying the breeze. At the same time, the cannon visible on the walkway would have been a potent reminder of the historic military role of Fort Hamilton, which served as a training center during the American Civil War.

Fig. 9
William Merritt Chase (1849–1916)
BATH BEACH: A SKETCH (BENSONHURST), ca. 1887
Oil on canvas, 27 x 49¾ in.
Parrish Art Museum, Southampton, NY, Gift of Mrs. Robert Malcolm Littlejohn, Littlejohn Collection, 1961.4.24

Another influential chronicler of modern upper- and middle-class urban life was Childe Hassam, who, while in Paris from 1886 to 1889, embraced the Impressionists' concern with capturing the effects of sunlight on his modern subjects.[5] During the 1890s, he created more than fifty paintings and pastels depicting New York's fashionable residential neighborhoods,[6] scenes such as *Spring Morning in the Heart of the City* (fig. 10) that celebrate the grand, bustling spaces of Gilded Age Manhattan. For Hassam, Chase, and their contemporaries such as Guy Wiggins, New York was a place inhabited by the wealthy, where streets were clean and wide, commercial establishments upscale, and there was a park around every corner. In Wiggins' *A February Storm in New York* (fig. 11), the falling snow softens the city's harsh outlines and obscures its details, creating the effect of muting the urban din. It is difficult to reconcile the New York City these artists chose to paint with the one exposed by Jacob Riis in his influential book *How the Other Half Lives*, which was a bestseller from the time of its publication in 1890 and made clear the hardships faced by the city's poor.

In 1896 Hassam returned to Europe, spending the summer and autumn of 1897 on the Brittany coast in Pont Aven, where he painted *At the Quai, Pont Aven* (fig. 3).[7]

Pont Aven was a well-known artist's colony frequented by both French and American artists who found irresistible subject matter in the area's quaint stone buildings and picturesque peasants attired in traditional Breton costume. Hassam painted more than a dozen canvases in Pont Aven, many of which were enlivened by these timeless figures—unusual subject matter for a painter who generally favored modern urban subjects.[8]

Visiting small hamlets and artist's colonies in Europe, and attempting to recreate them back home in the United States, was a major component of American Impressionist painting. The French village of Giverny was a particular draw for the American Impressionists who were lured by the hope of encountering Claude Monet, its most famous resident, and the promise of plenty of scenic plein-air landscape painting.[9] In the late nineteenth and early twentieth centuries, American artists flocked to the small village in Normandy, transforming it into a colorful and thriving artists' community centered around the famous Hôtel Baudy,

Above: Fig. 12
Claude Monet (1840–1926)
BRIDGE AT DOLCEACQUA, 1884
Oil on canvas, 25 9/16 x 32 1/8 in.
Sterling and Francine Clark Art Institute, Williamstown, Massachusetts. Gift of Richard and Edna Salomon, 1985.11

Opposite bottom: Fig. 11
Guy Wiggins (1883–1962)
A FEBRUARY STORM IN NEW YORK, 1919
Oil on pressed board, 12 in. x 9 in.
Florence Griswold Museum, Gift of Adelaide Dana Bagley in memory of Edwin Gates Bagley, 1992.1

15

Fig. 5 (*see page 9*)
Theodore Robinson (1852–1896)
**JOSEPHINE IN
THE GARDEN (AT THE
FOUNTAIN)**, ca. 1890
Oil on canvas, 32¼ x 26⅛ in.
*Arkell Museum Collection,
Gift of Bartlett Arkell, 1946*

where they enjoyed the spirit of camaraderie that was the most important aspect of the colony for many.

Theodore Robinson, the Vermont-born son of a Methodist minister, spent much of his career in France, where he painted primarily landscapes and female figures influenced by a succession of more academic styles before embracing Impressionism in 1888 in Giverny. There he painted alongside Monet—Robinson was among the only American painters to have met the French master—and adopted his Impressionist style.[10] In an article on Monet, Robinson praised the artist's use of color in canvases such as *Bridge at Dolceacqua* (fig. 12), asserting "That there is more color in nature than the average viewer is aware of….the modern eye is being educated to distinguish a complexity of shades and varieties of color before unknown."[11]

Robinson's painting *Josephine in the Garden (At the Fountain)* (fig. 5), in which he depicts his model, Josephine Trognon, in Monet's famed landscape, is representative of the style and subject matter of his Giverny canvases, which many consider his finest works. Both it and *Autumn Sunlight (In the Woods)* (fig. 13) also demonstrate the strong sense of design in his compositions, which was characteristic of his style throughout his career. Robinson often used photographs as a tool to record specific effects, particularly for his figurative works.

Left: Fig. 13
Theodore Robinson (1852–1896)
**AUTUMN SUNLIGHT
(IN THE WOODS)**, 1888
Oil on canvas, 18⅛ x 21¾ in.
*Florence Griswold Museum,
Gift of The Hartford Steam
Boiler Inspection and Insurance
Company, 2002.2.114*

Opposite: Fig. 14
John Henry Twachtman (1853–1902)
A BREEZY DAY, ca. 1885–1900
Oil on canvas, 20 x 16 in.
*Arkell Museum at Canajoharie,
Gift of Bartlett Arkell, 1928*

On frequent trips he made back to New York, and after settling there permanently in 1892, Robinson did much to familiarize his fellow American artists with Impressionism, and is credited with influencing his close friends J. Alden Weir and John Henry Twachtman (fig. 14) to adopt the style. Twachtman was in Paris from 1883 to 1885, studying painting at the Académie Julian and meeting fellow artists Hassam, Benson, and Tarbell. He spent the latter part of the 1880s in New York, where he worked in a Tonalist style characterized by unpopulated landscape scenes—often including evidence of human presence such as a path or fence—painted with traditional studio techniques using subtle gradations of unified, subdued tones. In 1889 he bought a seventeen-acre farm in the Cos Cob section of Greenwich, Connecticut, where Robinson and Weir frequently joined him for painting excursions, and where he began painting in the Impressionist style.

In 1891 Twachtman began holding summer classes in Cos Cob that attracted students from nearby New York City who wished to experiment with painting out of doors. The most famous was Ernest Lawson, whose canvas *Connecticut Landscape* (fig. 15) demonstrates his early commitment to Impressionism. Lawson and others found room, board, and the companionship of fellow artists at the Holley House, which became the center of an art colony that thrived through 1920. In the words of Susan

Fig. 15
Ernest Lawson (1873–1939)
CONNECTICUT LANDSCAPE, ca. 1902–1904
Oil on canvas, 24⅛ x 24⅛ in.
Florence Griswold Museum, Gift of The Hartford Steam Boiler Inspection and Insurance Company, 2002.1.84

Larkin, the colony's chief chronicler, for the American Impressionists, "Cos Cob in the 1890s was as important to them as Argenteuil in the 1870s had been to Monet, Renoir, and Manet. It was their testing ground for new styles and new themes. As they encouraged one another to challenge artistic conventions, they benefited from the stimulus of the writers, editors, and journalists who were also members of the art colony."[12]

The small communities that line the Connecticut shore proved a perfect locale for artists, offering the pleasures and scenic attractions of a rural landscape environment within easy proximity of both New York City and Boston. In the summer of 1900 an art colony emerged in Old

Fig. 16
William Merritt Chase (1849–1916)
THE POT HUNTER, ca. 1894
Oil on canvas, 16¼ x 24⅛ in.
Parrish Art Museum, Southampton,
NY, Purchase Fund and
Gift of Mr. Frank Sherer, 1974.5

Fig. 17
Childe Hassam (1859–1935)
**AMAGANSETT,
LONG ISLAND,
NEW YORK**, 1920

Oil on canvas, 20 x 30 in.
*Munson-Williams-Proctor Arts
Institute, museum purchase, 58.7*

Lyme, about ninety miles up the coast from Cos Cob. Centered around the boarding house of Florence Griswold, whose first artist-boarder was the American Tonalist painter Henry Ward Ranger in 1899, the colony became a bastion of American Impressionism after Childe Hassam discovered it in 1903. Artists including Willard Metcalf and William Chadwick began flocking to Old Lyme, where they created canvases such as Chadwick's *Irises* (fig. 2) that celebrate the beauty of the landscape.

The rural landscape, beaches, and quaint villages at the eastern tip of Long Island were also a draw for painters wishing to escape New York City in the summer. In 1891 Chase began painting and teaching at the Shinnecock Hills Summer School of Art, which flourished until 1902 and was the most famous school for outdoor work in the United States (fig. 16), the perfect analogue to French art colonies such as Giverny, Grez, and Barbizon. Hassam spent each summer from 1920 to 1934 painting in East Hampton and its surrounding hamlets, where he created canvases such as *Amagansett, Long Island, New York* (fig. 17) that celebrate the area's colonial history and quintessential Americanness. Indeed it wasn't just the congenial company, affordable accommodations, respite from city life, and opportunity for plein-air landscape painting that attracted artists from New York and Boston to towns such as Cos Cob and Old Lyme, and later Provincetown and Gloucester, Massachusetts; Cornish, New Hampshire; and Newport, Rhode Island. It was also the rusticity and small-town feel of these New England locales, which provided ample subject matter for paintings that would appeal to collectors.

Among Hassam's finest works are images of the churches that were landmarks of many of the colonial towns he frequented. In their analysis of *Provincetown* (fig. 20), the art historians H. Barbara Weinberg, Doreen Bolger, and David Park Curry argue that Hassam may have had a nationalistic, even patriotic agenda, for the painting.[13] His decision to emphasize the church, its steeple towering over the village and harbor, can certainly be seen as a reflection of the Puritan values he espoused over the course

Fig. 2 (*see page 2*)
William Chadwick (1879–1962)
IRISES, n.d.
Oil on canvas, 25 x 30 in.
Florence Griswold Museum,
Gift of Elizabeth Chadwick O'Connell,
1975.7.5

of his career. Also noteworthy are the ships Hassam chose to paint in Provincetown Harbor, which include sailing pleasure craft rather than working schooners or steamboats. These aesthetic choices reflect both his own and his clients' desire to find pre-industrial charm in New England villages they visited.

Likewise, Twachtman's view of *Gloucester Harbor* (fig. 6), which he probably painted in 1900, the first of the three summers he spent in Gloucester, subsumes the working life of the seaport town into a delicately lacy, atmospheric scene. By the time Twachtman was painting there, Gloucester was the site of a significant shipbuilding and fishing center that in the late nineteenth century saw an influx of Portuguese and Italian immigrant laborers. Yet Twachtman chose to romanticize the seaport. The foreground of trees and foliage, and high vantage point, suggest a rural scene of hills rolling down to the shore. The delicate pier angles into the harbor of placid blue water punctuated by gleaming white sails. The distant shore is equally verdant. A similar tendency toward nostalgia is evident in Allen Tucker's *Ice Harvesting* (fig. 18), a winter scene that chronicles not just a changing industry but a simpler way of life in New England that was disappearing before people's eyes. While Twachtman and Tucker were certainly experimenting with avant-garde aesthetic strategies, they were also ignoring many realities of turn-of-the-century experience. In Twachtman's Gloucester scene there is little evidence of laborers or industry—the fish canneries, steam-powered ships, power lines, trolley cars and tracks, and other realities that drove the modern life in the town—but much to suggest why artists and tourists found the area so appealing.

The convergence of artists and tourists is noteworthy. On the Isles of Shoals off the coast of Maine and New Hampshire, Celia Thaxter encouraged the sale of paintings made by her boarders, notably Hassam, which she displayed on the walls of her boarding house on the island of Appledore. In the 1880s and early 1890s, her parlor became a place where art was produced and enjoyed, as well as an active commercial gallery where works were sold to visitors seeking a souvenir of the time they spent there.

Like Thaxter, Florence Griswold also encouraged the sale of her boarder's paintings. One guidebook announced that the Griswold House contained "many framed pictures and other works of art which the visitor can have for a consideration."[14] The Old Lyme art colonists themselves

Fig. 18
Allen Tucker (1866–1939)
ICE HARVESTING, 1910
Oil on canvas, 20 x 30 in.
Fenimore Art Museum,
Gift of Allen Tucker Memorial
Photograph by Richard Walker

also mounted exhibitions of their work, the first of which was held in the local library in 1902. The Hartford newspaper reported that the library was crowded by visitors from "Hartford, New Haven, Middletown, New York, New London, Boston, Chicago, Springfield, and other places."[15] In 1912, the art colonists in Cos Cob organized as the Greenwich Society of Artists, mounting exhibitions at Greenwich's Bruce Museum marketed toward the town's wealthy residents and summer visitors. And in East Gloucester, William and Emmeline Atwood opened the Gallery-on-the-Moors in 1916, which featured annual exhibitions of paintings and prints by artists working in Gloucester.[16] Encouraged by these and other spontaneous summertime galleries, it is no surprise that the Impressionists chose to focus on the picturesque aspects of the locales they frequented. They captured images they knew would appeal to tourists in the same way that Chase and Hassam painted the city the way collectors preferred to have their world recorded—glossing over the darker, seamier aspects of progress.

Fig. 20. Childe Hassam (1859–1935). **PROVINCETOWN**, 1900. Oil on canvas, 24⅛ x 22⅛ in. *Arkell Museum at Canajoharie, Gift of Bartlett Arkell, 1929*

In American Impressionism, what seemed innovative in the 1880s became self-consciously conservative after about 1900. It wasn't until the group of Realist painters known as The Eight came along in 1908 that a modern style merged with a modern way of viewing the world. The somber palette of William Glackens's 1906 work *Under the Trees, Luxembourg Gardens* (fig. 19) anticipates the stylistic transformation he and his colleagues in The Eight would undertake. Led by Robert Henri, and also known as the Ashcan School for the gritty urban subjects they illustrated, the group posed a significant challenge to the American Impressionists, whose work increasingly came to be seen by critics and collectors as retardataire. In the words of a writer for the *New York Sun* in 1916, "'The Ten' are impressionists who once banded together in a sort of protest against the Academy. They were the 'protest' of a generation ago, and as far as the protest concerns ideals it must be allowed that they won the point long since."[17] While Hassam, Tarbell, and Benson and a handful of their acolytes would persist in painting genteel women in well-appointed interiors well into the 20th century (fig. 21), the introduction of Post-Impressionism, Fauvism, Expressionism, Cubism, and other modernist art movements at the Armory Show in New York in 1913, followed by the outbreak of World War I in Europe the following year, revealed just how obsolete the Impressionists' nostalgic and optimistic way of seeing had become.

MEGAN HOLLOWAY FORT, Ph.D., *Art Historian*

Fig. 21
Lilian Westcott Hale (1881–1963)
WOMAN RESTING, ca. 1942
Oil on canvas, 20 x 14 in.
*Florence Griswold Museum,
Gift of The Hartford Steam
Boiler Inspection and Insurance
Company, 2002.1.171*

American Impressionist Paintings from Macbeth Gallery to Canajoharie

DIANE E. FORSBERG

WHEN THE DOORS OF THE ART GALLERY at the Canajoharie Library (now known as the Arkell Museum) opened to the public in 1927, visitors were greeted with a sky-lit room filled with painted copies of seventeenth-century European masterpieces and original paintings by American artists hanging side-by-side on the walls (fig. 22). This seemingly odd mix was compiled by Bartlett Arkell (1860–1946), the founder and first president of the Beech-Nut Packing Company. Arkell acquired copies of paintings by artists such as Rembrandt and Vermeer with the belief that the replicas could bring the enriching experiences he had encountered in European museums to the village of Canajoharie. He simultaneously purchased original works by American artists to inspire regional and national pride in the people of his hometown.

Most of the paintings Bartlett Arkell donated to the Canajoharie Library and Art Gallery were never part of his personal collection. There is some overlap in the names of artists in the two collections, but a comparison of subject matter and styles shows that he had a different set of collecting criteria for the public and his personal use. Tonalism[1] and American Impressionism coexisted in the late nineteenth and early twentieth centuries, and paintings in both styles were exhibited and sold by art dealers when Arkell was purchasing art in the 1920s and 1930s. The paintings Arkell acquired for his personal enjoyment included a large number of Tonalist works. These paintings were darker and more somber than the bright Impressionist and Regionalist paintings he selected for the public. The Tonalist paintings—more about mood than place—did not provide Arkell with his ideal of what was "American" in American art. The Impressionist paintings he collected for the public embodied what Arkell wanted to share with Canajoharie's people—uplifting and cheerful scenes of America's unique architecture, people and landscape.

Fig. 22
CANAJOHARIE ART GALLERY
Looking east toward original library, mid- to late-1930s.
Original American Impressionist watercolors and pastels
by Melchers, Hassam, Prendergast and Benson installed
among American paintings and copies of works by Frans
Hals and Vermeer.

Fig. 23
BARTLETT ARKELL

Bartlett Arkell, the first President of the Beech-Nut Packaging Company, stands in front of the people he felt an obligation to support and culturally enrich. The Beech-Nut workers are dressed in their white uniforms on the left and other Canajoharie village inhabitants are on the right. *Arkell Museum at Canajoharie, 1996.1*

Almost all of the paintings in the Canajoharie Library and Art Gallery were purchased from Macbeth Gallery in New York City. Three men played a role in Macbeth Gallery's history and direction—William Macbeth (1851–1917), his son Robert Macbeth (1884–1940), and his nephew Robert McIntyre (1885– 1965). It was the second generation of men at Macbeth Gallery who developed a strong friendship with Bartlett Arkell and instilled in him a passion for American art. Under their guidance, the Canajoharie collection grew over two decades (1925–1946) to include paintings by most of the leading American realists and American Impressionist artists active during the late nineteenth and first half of the twentieth centuries.

William Macbeth opened his commercial New York City Gallery in 1892 to exhibit and sell American oil paintings and watercolors at a time when French and American Impressionists were still considered radicals. It was a risky business decision to open a gallery that did not sell traditional European art. Hudson River School paintings were no longer in great demand by industrialists, and no one was clamoring for more work by the next generation of American artists. Collectors purchased American art directly from the artist's studio, periodic exhibits of paintings at gentlemen's clubs, or from the National Academy exhibitions. They were accustomed to going to art dealers to buy European art—not American paintings.[2]

In 1895 Macbeth Gallery held Theodore Robinson's first one-man exhibition, which was well received by most critics, but not appreciated by the buying public. The *New York Sun* wrote: "Among the disciples of Impressionism in painting among our local artists none is more serious nor more worthy of consideration than Mr. Theodore Robinson ... Mr. Robinson has found his subjects in romantic places round about New York or in rural France. The essential characteristics are preserved significantly in either case, and it is perfectly plain, too, that Mr. Robinson has painted out of doors, and has put into his work impressions of a very personal sort... ."[3] The public was not as favorably impressed by the 33 works on display, and only one of Robinson's paintings sold at this exhibition. The buyer was the American Impressionist painter William Merritt Chase.[4] Among the unsold works in Robinson's first one-man show was *Normandy Farm*, an oil painting with the same title and subject as the Robinson watercolor (fig. 39) Arkell later purchased and had on exhibit when the Canajoharie Art Gallery opened in 1927. The failure of Robinson's one-man exhibition kept Macbeth Gallery from holding a second one-man show of the artist's works until 1943.

Fig. 24
Childe Hassam (1859–1935)
BRIDGE AT OLD LYME, 1908
Oil on canvas, 23⅝ x 25⅝ in.
Georgia Museum of Art,
University of Georgia;
Eva Underhill Memorial
Collection of American Art,
Gift of Alfred H. Holbrook, 1945.47
Not in exhibition

Most American Impressionists struggled to sell their art, and Robert Macbeth recalled that "The first American followers of the new idea, Twachtman, Robinson, Weir and Hassam, had brought their pictures back to an audience far from ready to receive them, and most of them got no attention until some years later."[5] Macbeth kept promoting these artists, and with time found a market for their work with private collectors and in the new American art museums. Macbeth was pleased to note that "American art and artists have decidedly come into their own...It was a brave collector who bought their work in 1892 cannot show a goodly representation of the best of them in 1922!"[6]

Bartlett Arkell's association with Macbeth Gallery predates his decision to create a gallery for Canajoharie. His first important purchase was in 1917 when William Macbeth persuaded him to pay more for a George Inness painting than he felt was suitable.[7] Once he owned the painting, Arkell found that he was very happy with his acquisition, and he started to procure other important paintings for his personal collection. He went on to share his new passion by purchasing paintings for the Canajoharie Library before the Gallery was added, but did not donate any Impressionist paintings until plans were well underway for the Canajoharie Art Gallery.

When Bartlett Arkell started to purchase works by American Impressionists, they were no longer avant-garde—they had become icons in the American art world. Childe Hassam was one of the best known living artists in America, and Arkell acquired at least seven works by Hassam from Macbeth Gallery. Childe Hassam's bold and brightly colored Impressionist painting *Bridge at Old Lyme*, 1908, (fig. 24) was hanging on the wall in the Canajoharie Art Gallery when it opened in 1927.[8] It was a breathtaking example of American Impressionism and the most modern painting on display in the Canajoharie Art Gallery.

Hassam had no interest in art styles coming from Europe after Impressionism. Bartlett Arkell may have shared Hassam's views, but there are no direct comments recorded from Arkell on the subject. The year the Canajoharie Art Gallery opened, Hassam was quoted in an interview complaining about Cubism and Futurism:

Fig. 1 (*see inside front cover*)
Childe Hassam (1859–1935)
AMERICAN ELM, 1905 (or 1903?)
Oil on canvas, 20⅛ x 14⅛ in.
Arkell Hall Foundation

Opposite bottom: Fig. 26
Childe Hassam (1859–1935)
BEACH AT GLOUCESTER, 1897
Watercolor on paper, 23½ x 28½ in.
Arkell Museum at Canajoharie,
Gift of Bartlett Arkell, 1933
Not in exhibition

Fig. 25
Childe Hassam (1859–1935)
CAPRI, 1897
Oil on canvas, 29 x 23 ¼ in.
*Addison Gallery, Phillips Academy,
Andover, Massachusetts,
Gift of Bartlett Arkell, Esq., 1930.382
Not in exhibition*

Arkell was never attracted to abstract art—he wanted paintings of places
and people that would inspire Gallery visitors to feel proud about the
American landscape and its inhabitants. *Provincetown* (fig. 20) was the
second Hassam painting Arkell acquired for the Canajoharie Art Gallery.
Provincetown, like many of Hassam's city and town views, features a
church steeple. Critics often praised Hassam paintings for their embod-
iment of American patriotic and religious values, and the church steeple
was seen as a testament to America as a godly country. The painting
also includes American elms that were referred to as the "tree of the
people" and seen as a symbol of America's past. [10] The symbolic mean-
ings associated with this tree would have been known to Arkell when
he purchased Hassam's painting entitled *American Elm* (fig. 1) for his
personal collection.

   Provincetown and *Bridge at Old Lyme* were loaned to Macbeth Gallery's April 1929 *Exhibition of Paintings by Childe Hassam*. About half
of the paintings in the exhibition were on loan and not for sale. Arkell
found two paintings to buy at this exhibition, but they were not sent to
the Gallery in Canajoharie. Arkell obtained *At the Quai, Pont Aven* (fig. 3)
for his personal collection and
donated *Capri* (fig. 25) to the
Addison Gallery at Phillips
Academy. It is important to
note that Arkell would later
purchase another Hassam for
the Canajoharie Art Gallery—
a watercolor entitled *Beach at
Gloucester* (fig. 26). Arkell gave
Canajoharie the Hassam works
that represented the American
towns frequently painted by
the American Impressionists,
and reserved the paintings of
French and Italian scenes for
his family's enjoyment and an
academic collection. [11]

In 1928, the year Canajoharie was celebrating its new Gallery, Arkell acquired Childe Hassam's pastel *Brush House* (fig. 27) for his granddaughter Mary Arkell. This work was included in Macbeth Gallery's exhibition "American Paintings for Home Decoration."[12] Macbeth often organized exhibitions to emphasize that American paintings were not just for museums or prosperous collectors. This exhibition catalog noted that "There is a too prevalent idea that only the very wealthy can afford to buy American paintings. This is due largely to the figures quoted at big exhibitions where, for the most part, the artists send their largest canvases, most of which are too big, both in size and price, for the consideration of the home owners of comparatively moderate incomes."[13]

Fig. 27
Childe Hassam (1859–1935)
BRUSH HOUSE, 1902
Pastel on paper, 18⅙ x 22⅛ in.
Arkell Museum at Canajoharie,
Given in loving memory
of Mary Arkell Price by her
husband, Robert M. Price
and their children, 1997
Not in exhibition

This pastel portrays the Brush House that stood across the road from the better known Holley House (now known as the Bush-Holly House). Both homes were summer residences for the artists who came to Cos Cob—and both were painted by Hassam several times. In reality, the Brush House was never as well cared for as the Bush-Holly House, but Hassam chose to omit all evidence of the Brush House's poor upkeep and presented it as an idealized summer retreat.[14] The American Impressionist artists J. Alden Weir and John Henry Twachtman also came to this summer art colony, and all three men were members of a group of artists known as The Ten.

The artists banded together as "The Ten American Painters" after they resigned from the Society of American Artists in 1897. Exhibitions held by the Society of American Artists were perceived by The Ten as too large, uneven in quality, and growing less open to Impressionist works. The Ten exhibited together from 1898–1919 at a wide variety of commercial galleries and public museums, but never as a complete group at the Macbeth Gallery. Nevertheless, paintings by these artists were often available at Macbeth Gallery where Arkell purchased works by the following members of The Ten: Childe Hassam, Frank Benson, Thomas Dewing, Edmund Tarbell, John H. Twachtman, J. Alden Weir, Willard Metcalf and William Merritt Chase (who joined the group after Twachtman's death).

The Arkell Museum owns two John Henry Twachtman paintings. *A Breezy Day* (also called *The Road*) (fig. 14) was acquired by Arkell in 1928, and it appeared as the frontispiece in "Magazine of American Art" in April 1929[15]—a testament to its high regard at the time. In 1939 Arkell bought Twachtman's *Gloucester Harbor* (fig. 6)—a more modern work than *A Breezy Day*. The earlier painting has the high-keyed color used by Impressionists, but the placement and design of the road and tree recall the style of earlier Barbizon artists. *Gloucester Harbor*, however, goes well beyond the work of French Barbizon and Impressionist artists to offer a new and modern approach to organizing the landscape.

During his life, Twachtman was admired by his fellow artists, but he did not gain the interest of the general public until the 1910s and 1920s. His paintings incorporated modern compositional elements that were not found in works by his contemporaries. The angles and geometry of the dock and buildings in *Gloucester Harbor* were quite radical, and made viewers who were more accustomed to Hudson River School landscapes uncomfortable with its lack of adherence to the established traditions of selecting and framing the landscape. Unlike American nineteenth-century paintings, it had a high horizon line painted on a square canvas with no trees framing the sides. Twachtman exhibited this and other paintings with the same title "Gloucester" in several exhibitions by The Ten. Twachtman hated the task of providing titles which has led to some confusion as he let others title his works for him.[16]

Edmund Charles Tarbell's painting *A Girl Crocheting* (fig. 28) arrived at the Canajoharie Library the same time as Twachtman's *Gloucester Harbor*.[17] *A Girl Crocheting*, however, displays a greater connection to Dutch seventeenth-century art than to French

Fig. 28
Edmund Tarbell (1862–1938)
A GIRL CROCHETING, 1904
Oil on canvas, 30¼ x 25¼ in.
Arkell Museum at Canajoharie,
Gift of Bartlett Arkell, 1939
Not in exhibition

Impressionist works. This painting fit in well with the Dutch copies Arkell commissioned for the new Gallery, especially Vermeer's *Reading Woman*. Tarbell created *A Girl Crocheting* in 1904—the year that the first American monograph on Vermeer was published. This was also the time when

Tarbell started to leave behind the bright high-keyed palette of the Impressionists in favor of the darker more somber tones he used to paint interior scenes with women. The painting was exhibited in a group show of The Ten at Montross Gallery where critics referred to it as the best painting, not only in the show, but of the season. The painting continued to garner praise when exhibited at six locations between 1905 and 1908, including the Worcester Art Museum, Pennsylvania Academy of Fine Arts, and the Corcoran Gallery of Art.[18] *A Girl Crocheting* was purchased by a fellow artist and friend of Tarbell's for $2,500 and sold for $16,000 in 1917—the highest price ever paid for an American painting. The painting was not as highly prized when Bartlett Arkell bought it in 1928 and had it insured for only $1,800. In September 1940 the painting was loaned to the Carnegie Institute and the borrower pointed out that the painting had been insured for $10,000 when it was awarded First Prize in the 1909 Carnegie International, and later insured for $25,000 when it was exhibited at the Carnegie in 1922.[19] Macbeth Gallery revised the insurance value up to $3,500—still much lower than its apparent worth from 1917 through 1922. The diminishing value of the Tarbell painting reflects more than the public's changing opinion of this particular work—it is a sign of collectors' waning interest in American Impressionist works at the very time Arkell started to buy them for the Canajoharie Art Gallery.

Bartlett Arkell bought William Merritt Chase's *The Connoisseur-In the Studio Corner* (fig. 4), from Macbeth Gallery in 1927, but it took over a decade for the work to arrive at the Gallery and go on display. Arkell wrote to the curator in 1939 that the Chase painting "somehow got to my home and has been there a long time. I know the Gallery will be delighted with this picture, the finest Chase ever painted."[20] When the Chase painting arrived at the Gallery it entered under the erroneous title *The Studio Corner* and was exhibited as *In the Studio Corner*. The incorrect titles drastically changed how visitors and some art historians viewed and interpreted the painting. The title *In the Studio Corner* encouraged viewers to see the figure of the woman as one of the many beautiful objects in the corner of Chase's studio. The sitter was actually Chase's future sister-in-law, Virginia Gerson. She was typical of the women who spent time in Chase's 10th Street Studio in New York City—a well educated art student, connoisseur, and art patron.[21]

Fig. 4 (*see page 6*)
William Merritt Chase (1849–1916)
THE CONNOISSEUR-IN THE STUDIO CORNER, ca. 1885
Oil on canvas, 20⅛ x 24⅛ in.
Arkell Museum at Canajoharie, Gift of Bartlett Arkell, 1945

Another member of The Ten, Willard Metcalf, is not represented in the collection that Arkell assembled for the Canajoharie Art Gallery. Metcalf's brilliant *The Red Maple* (fig. 29) was, however, on public display at the Beech-Nut building, and frequently brought across the street and exhibited in the Canajoharie Art Gallery.[22] Paintings owned by Arkell also moved between the Beech-Nut Packing company buildings and the Wagner Hotel (later known as the Beech-Nut Hotel). *The Red Maple* was in the Gallery when a *Catalogue of the Permanent Collection* was printed in the early 1930s.[23] The *Catalogue* opened with an essay by Royal Corissoz— an art historian and art critic for the *New York Herald Tribune* who decried modernism in favor of realism. Corissoz stated in his introduction that "the subject of American art is a large one. But the Canajoharie Gallery throws upon it a most revealing light." He praised the collection for "the persistence of good workmanship, the loyalty of our painters to the truths of nature, and their triumphant expression of themselves in their transcripts of fact."

The back of the *Catalogue of the Permanent Collection* included a list of all of the "Other Paintings in the Library, Wagner Hotel and at the Beechnut Packing," followed by a list of paintings in the "Recreation Hall." After this publication, Macbeth Gallery continued to assist with the printing of Canajoharie Art Gallery catalogs (actually simple checklists with no introduction) and they would routinely list paintings on display at other locations around town with the ones on view at the Gallery. These small catalogs attest to the idea that Arkell was not just building a museum collection to share with his peers; he was acquiring art to enrich the lives of his employees and village residents, and he wanted them to find art where they worked and throughout the village.

Frank Benson's *Black Ducks* and Theodore Robinson's *Normandy Farm* (fig. 39) were among the first works on paper to enter the Canajoharie Art Gallery. In the 1930s Arkell acquired additional American Impressionist pastels and watercolors by Childe Hassam, Gari Melchers, and Maurice Prendergast. These works on paper were installed in the Canajoharie Art Gallery alongside oil paintings by Winslow Homer and the copies of European paintings. Winslow Homer and the American Impressionists were among the first artists to create watercolors as finished

Fig. 29
Willard Metcalf (1858–1925)
THE RED MAPLE, 1920
Oil on canvas, 26 x 29 in.
Arkell Hall Foundation

works of arts, rather than studies for oil paintings. At first, critics did not see these works on paper as worthy of museum display, but no one questioned their gallery placement next to oil paintings in the 1930s. Reviews of the Canajoharie Art Gallery in the 1930s frequently listed these works among the highlights of the collection.

Paintings in the Canajoharie Art Gallery collection include several important second generation American Impressionists. Ernest Lawson's *Winter Twilight—Brooklyn Bridge*, 1933 (fig. 31) entered the museum collection in 1934 as a gift of the artist through Macbeth Gallery. Lawson was a follower of Twachtman and Weir, and like the French Impressionist Claude Monet he often returned to the same landscape subject to paint it again. Lawson, however, was not as interested in capturing different times of day; he was re-examining the Brooklyn Bridge (fig. 30) during different seasons or from a slightly different vantage point.

Edward Redfield was one of the best known second-generation Impressionists, so it was not surprising to find his *Sleigh Bells* (fig. 32) in the new Canajoharie Art Gallery when it first opened. Redfield's reputation was well established by this time, and his work had been shown regularly at Macbeth Gallery since the early 1900s.[24] Redfield painted this street scene in New Hope, Pennsylvania many times, and at least four of his paintings are titled *Sleigh Bells*.[25] Like Lawson's paintings of the Brooklyn Bridge, Redfield returned to this scene on Main Street in New Hope (fig. 33) from a slightly different perspective. Winter was Redfield's favorite season—he was not capturing different seasonal effects, he was exploring vantage points.

Fig. 30
Ernest Lawson (1873–1939)
BROOKLYN BRIDGE, 1917–1920
Oil on canvas, 20⅜ x 24 in.
Daniel J. Terra Collection, 1992.43
Not in exhibition

Fig. 31
Ernest Lawson (1873–1939)
**WINTER TWILIGHT –
BROOKLYN BRIDGE**, 1932
Oil on canvas, 17½ x 22½
*Arkell Museum at Canajoharie,
Gift of the artist, 1933*

The Pennsylvania Academy gave Redfield a one-man exhibition in 1909 and offered the praise that "Among the men whose work may be considered typical of our time no one is more characteristically American than Mr. Redfield."[26] Referring to an artist's work as "American" was a form of praise—but its exact meaning is not always so clear. Generally, calling the painting "American" was noting that the artist had captured some unique aspect of the American landscape in his painting. "American"

also meant that the painting style was not too derivative of the work of the French Impressionists. It implied that the artist had learned the techniques by studying abroad and then gone on to make the style his own— or to make it "American." The concept of learning from Europe, and then using that knowledge to create something distinctly American was not new, and it was something that Bartlett Arkell and Ivy League College-educated men[27] of his generation embraced in their own lives and businesses. This is the idea behind Arkell's decision to exhibit copies of great European masters alongside original American art in the Canajoharie Art Gallery.

Many Americans lost interest in the Impressionists after the crash of the stock market, and by the 1930s Impressionism was no longer in vogue. From the mid-1930s to the mid-1940s the Modern Museum of Art (now known as MoMA) was acquiring works by Paul Klee and Max Weber— not the first or second generation of American Impressionists. Robert Macbeth blasted the Modern about its collecting choices in his November 1930 publication of *Art Notes*. He urged American museums to collect "sane" American art[28]—meaning the American Impressionists he was exhibiting at his Gallery. Macbeth had a loyal collector in Bartlett Arkell who had no interest in modern abstract art and continued to collect Impressionist works from Macbeth Gallery.

Robert Macbeth died suddenly in 1940, and from 1941 to 1943 Arkell purchased mostly Winslow Homer watercolors and oil paintings under the guidance of Robert McIntyre who had taken charge of Macbeth Gallery. Arkell set up a drawing account in 1941 to help support the Gallery after Robert Macbeth's death. The account was used to make several

purchases and trades. One of his purchases was *The Brook* (fig. 34), an Impressionist painting by Theodore Robinson. *The Brook* arrived at the Canajoharie Art Gallery in January 1942 along with an oil painting by Winslow Homer.[29]

Robinson's *The Brook* is not a bright sun-dappled Impressionist view like the ones he usually created under the influence of Monet in Giverny. It is a shaded scene with broad short strokes of green and blue paint that remind the viewer that this is a painting on canvas, not a framed view of a landscape. The painting has no horizon line and the trees reach the top of the canvas, which further emphasizes the flat picture plane.

Fig. 34
Theodore Robinson (1852–1896)
THE BROOK, ca. 1891
Oil on canvas, 20 x 21 ½ in.
Mead Art Museum,
Amherst College,
Amherst, Massachusetts,
Gift of Charles H. Morgan,
AC 1968.26
Not in exhibition

Robinson may have ventured too close to abstraction with this painting for it to fit in with Bartlett Arkell's collection of American landscape views of farmland and villages that often recalled life in the Mohawk Valley. In 1943 Macbeth Gallery borrowed back *The Brook* for its second one-man show of Theodore Robinson's work. In the thank you letter for this loan, McIntyre mentions that *The Brook* "was a beautiful addition to the exhibition, and picked out for mention by several critics."[30] The painting did not stay in the Canajoharie collection, it was sent back to Macbeth Gallery less than two years later and the money was used to purchase another painting.

In 1945 Arkell purchased J. Alden Weir's *Summer Landscape, Connecticut*, (fig. 36). Prior to this time, Arkell had acquired Weir's *Still Life, Roses* for the Gallery. *Summer Landscape, Connecticut* is an impressionist scene that shows a man in a road which winds back around a house in the middle-ground. It was created with the conventions of traditional landscape painting—receding space, horizon line and sky—in contrast to the J. Alden Weir painting *Black Birch Rock* (fig. 35) that Arkell had in his personal collection and kept in his office at Beech-Nut Packing Company.[31] *Back Birch Rock* is painted in a consistent tone of light colors that tend to flatten the landscape and create a harmony of spring colors rather than a picture of a place.

Arkell also purchased very different works by John Singer Sargent for his family and the public collections. He acquired *Head of an Italian Woman* for the Canajoharie Art Gallery—a remarkable portrait—but not an impressionist work. For his family collection he bought the watercolor

Trees on a Hillside in Majorca, 1908, which demonstrates Sargent's brash brushwork that was seen by some at the time as unfinished—but praised by others for its spontaneity.

Theodore Robinson's *Josephine in the Garden* (*At the Fountain*) (fig. 5) was among the last works Arkell purchased from Macbeth Gallery before he died in 1946. The painting is filled with sun and shadows, and features a young woman with watering cans near a fountain. This painting had the narrative content and sunlight that had been missing in *The Brook*. *Josephine in the Garden* (*At the Fountain*) depicts Robinson's model, Josephine Tognon, in Claude Monet's hometown of Giverny, France. Claude Monet became Robinson's friend and was the reason Robinson and other American artists traveled to Giverny to paint. Monet wrote to Robinson in 1891 "we see some carefree and colorful people, your compatriots "checking" on the start of the spring. Spring is indeed on its way and I'm sure it won't be long until you come back to your little house here."[32] Bartlett Arkell, however, was not concerned with the painting's French subject matter—he was interested in the rustic farm and village image that was akin to works by Winslow Homer already in the Canajoharie Art Gallery collection. Robinson, in fact, admired Winslow Homer and owned one of his small paintings—a picture of a woman collecting wheat off the ground entitled *Wheat Gatherer*, 1867 (Frye Art Museum collection, Seattle).[33]

Fig. 35
J. Alden Weir (1852–1919)
BLACK BIRCH ROCK, n.d.
Oil on canvas, 23¼ x 35¼ in.
Arkell Hall Foundation
Not in exhibition

Fig. 36
J. Alden Weir (1852–1919)
SUMMER LANDSCAPE, CONNECTICUT, n.d.
Oil on canvas, 20⅛ x 24⅛ in.
Arkell Museum at Canajoharie, Gift of Bartlett Arkell, 1945

Josephine in the Garden (*At the Fountain*), and a watercolor, *Normandy Farm* (fig. 39), acquired for the museum's opening two decades earlier, were both created by Theodore Robinson using photographic studies as guides for the composition and placement of figures, foliage and architectural forms (fig. 38). Using photographs as a starting point probably added to the realism appreciated by Bartlett Arkell. Robinson noted in a letter to a family member that "Painting directly from nature is difficult as things do not remain the same, the camera helps retain the picture in your mind."[34] Robinson often placed a grid on his cyanotypes or albumen prints as a guide to transfer the composition onto canvas. Arkell was not aware of Robinson's use of photographs and would have thought that both works were painted *en plein air* without the aid of a camera. Robinson's brushwork, in both the pastel and the oil painting, were created with spontaneous and broken strokes that epitomize French Impressionism. Robinson did not speak publicly about his use of photographs, and was photographed painting out-of-doors (fig. 37) more than once, for promotional purposes.

Bartlett Arkell was not consciously collecting examples of American Impressionism, The Ten or The Eight, or trying to amass an encyclopedic collection that traced the history of American art—he was collecting American art that celebrated this nation's landscape and people. This idea about American art was promoted in Macbeth Gallery's *Art Notes* and exhibition catalogs.

In 1953 Robert McIntyre reviewed the Canajoharie Library art collection and created a list of the strengths and weaknesses based mostly on the idea of developing a collection that included all of the major American art movements and best known artists from the colonial period up through The Eight. Under the category of "Impressionists" McIntyre noted "You have Twachtman, Robinson, Hassam, Lawson, Prendergast and Weir. To these should be added Mary Cassatt."[35] Mary Cassatt was one of the first Americans to go abroad and paint with the French Impressionists. Cassatt played a major role in bringing

Fig. 38
**HOUSE AND GARDEN
WITH FIGURE**, n.d.
Albumen print
*Terra Foundation for the Arts,
Gift of Mr. Ira Spanierman,
C1985.1.15*
Not in exhibition

Fig. 39
Theodore Robinson (1852–1896)
NORMANDY FARM, ca. 1891
Watercolor and gouache
on paper, 13⅞ x 16⅞ in.
*Arkell Museum at Canajoharie,
Gift of Bartlett Arkell, 1947*
Not in exhibition

French Impressionists, particularly her friend and mentor Degas, to the
attention of American collectors. But she was not one of the Impressionists featured at Macbeth Gallery while Arkell was purchasing works for
his Gallery. In late July 1958 a special meeting was held at the Canajoharie
Library and Art Gallery to vote on "one of Mary Cassatt paintings pres-
ently hanging in the gallery."[36] The trustees selected Mary Cassatt's pastel
Portrait of a Woman now titled *Portrait of Mathilde Valiet* (fig. 40).[37]

41

Elizabeth Grammer, one of the Library board members, was ecstatic about the purchase and wrote to the board president about a conversation she had with Mrs. Breeskin, an authority on Mary Cassatt (fig. 44), and the first woman to direct a major American art museum—the Baltimore Museum of Art. Grammer wrote that Adelyn Breeskin "reminded me,

Mary Cassatt, following Monet and Degas, was largely responsible for reviving interest in pastel as a medium." She added a postscript to her letter: "it's the most exciting acquisition the gallery has made in some years…. Lots of people don't even know about the gallery and sometimes I think those who do are inclined to think our collection static, with never any new additions."[38] There is no indication in the correspondence about the Cassatt purchase that anyone had noticed the meager representation of women artists in the Canajoharie Art Gallery collection, and the need to fill this void. Breeskin wrote to the Canajoharie Art Gallery curator almost a decade after the acquisition with the news that the sitter may be "Miss Cassatt's companion—maid Mathilde Valiet—although it is probably better not to entitle it so, since it is just a guess."[39] The painting title was changed after this letter to *Portrait of Mathilde Valiet*.

McIntyre also listed William Glackens as one of the artists that should be acquired for the Canajoharie Art Gallery, but he included him under the category of "The Eight" rather than "Impressionist." Macbeth Gallery may be best remembered today for being the first to exhibit The Eight (also known as the Ashcan School) in 1908. The Eight shocked the public with their choice of urban subjects that included the everyday life of the poor in the city's streets and back alleys. Most of The Eight spent time in France and were in some way influenced by Impressionism during their careers. By the time of Arkell's death, William Glackens was the only member of The Eight not in the Canajoharie collection. Discussions went on for years between Macbeth Gallery and the curator of the Canajoharie Art Gallery about the purchase of a Glackens, "a good one,"[40] but the Glackens' painting *Beach at Nova Scotia* (fig. 41) was not acquired until 1958—five years after Macbeth Gallery had closed—so the work was purchased from Kraushaar Galleries.

Glackens' painting includes adults and young children engaged in leisure activities on the beach—a popular subject for Impressionist artists. This is the same theme as the watercolor *Revere Beach* (fig. 43) (in the Canajoharie Art Gallery collection since 1935) painted by Maurice Prendergast, a fellow member of The Eight. Each artist, however, had a very different approach to painting. Prendergast's watercolor is a decorative pattern of rocks and figures where design takes precedence over the subject.

The figures in Glackens' *Beach at Nova Scotia* are deftly rendered with bold strokes of paint that convey each figure's social standing and beach activity. Close inspection does not reveal facial features, but these are not looked-for and would interfere with the scene as a whole, which joyfully captures a day on the beach. The variety of participants on the beach include: a young child with a large white hat petting a dog, a couple looking out at the sail boats, an African American maid in white hat and apron kneeling on the grass so she can care for her young charge, a white woman in her straw hat pushing a stroller with a bonnet-clad toddler, and a man with his arm held high as if about to catch a ball.[41]

Fig. 41
William Glackens (1870–1938)
BEACH AT NOVA SCOTIA, 1910
Oil on canvas, 18 x 30 in.
Arkell Museum at Canajoharie,
museum purchase, 1958

The Cassatt portrait and the Glackens's watercolor were the last Impressionist works purchased by the Canajoharie Library and Art Gallery. The Gallery (fig. 42) was expanded to a museum of six galleries in 2007 and the name changed to The Arkell Museum at Canajoharie. The name change honors not only Bartlett Arkell, but also his sister Bertelle Arkell Barbour who established the Arkell Hall Foundation that paid for the new museum building. Bartlett Arkell did not want a gallery in his name—he wanted to provide a gallery filled with inspirational art that his Beech-Nut workers and all Canajoharie residents would view as their own.

Impressionist works in this collection celebrate the good life found in American homes, towns, farmlands and summer retreats. This was the positive message about American life that Bartlett Arkell wanted to share with the village of Canajoharie. It was also the image of Canajoharie that he skillfully marketed along with his Beech-Nut food, candy, and gum. While very little of what Arkell thought about Canajoharie Library's collection of Impressionist paintings was ever recorded in his correspondence or interviews, we do know how Arkell linked artist-created images with ideas to market Beech-Nut products. Words like "clean" and "bright" appeared in Beech-Nut ads alongside painted views of the Mohawk Valley. Hassam's *Provincetown* (fig. 20), Twachtman's *Gloucester Harbor* (fig. 6), Weir's *Summer Landscape, Connecticut* (fig. 36), Metcalf's *The Red Maple* (fig. 29) and the other Impressionist works Arkell collected share this same image of a "clean" and "bright" America. Arkell did not use his collection to bolster his position in society. But he clearly used art to help him market

Fig. 42
**CANAJOHARIE
ART GALLERY**, early 1928
Redfield's *Sleigh Bells* is the winter landscape over the fireplace on the left. Other American Impressionist works on display in 1928, but not in the photograph, included Childe Hassam's *Old Bridge at Lyme*, and Theodore Robinson's *Normandy Farm*. The largest painting in the Gallery is Martin J. Kopershoek's (1880–1935) *Copy of Rembrandt's The Nightwatch*, 1927.

Fig. 43
Maurice Prendergast (1861–1924)
REVERE BEACH, ca. 1902
Watercolor on paper, 14 x 20¼ in.
*Arkell Museum at Canajoharie, Gift of Bartlett Arkell
Not in exhibition*

Fig. 20 (*see page 24*)
Childe Hassam (1859–1935)
PROVINCETOWN, 1900
Oil on canvas, 24⅛ x 22⅛ in.
Arkell Museum at Canajoharie,
Gift of Bartlett Arkell, 1929

his beliefs regarding all that was good in American middle-class life. The American Impressionists who supported this vision of the landscape and modern life are at the heart of the Arkell Museum collection, and Arkell's ideals and legacy are reflected in the masterpieces he collected.

DIANE E. FORSBERG, *Deputy Director and Chief Curator,*
Arkell Museum at Canajoharie, New York

GEORGE BRUESTLE (1871–1939)

UNTITLED WINTER LANDSCAPE. n.d. Oil on artist's board mounted on cardboard, 3 x 4 in.
Florence Griswold Museum, Gift of the Estate of Mary Griswold Steube 1998.7.3

Bruestle was a stalwart member of the art colony at Old Lyme, Connecticut. Though he lived in a nearby house with his wife and son, rather than boarding at Florence Griswold's house with his artist friends, he was active in colony activities from the beginning and served as secretary of the Lyme Art Association in 1923. Like many of the painters in this exhibition, he spent his winters in New York where he was equally engaged in a number of artist organizations, including the Salmagundi and National Arts clubs. This group of landscapes reflects the range of Bruestle's talent for capturing the changing light and mood of the Connecticut landscape over seasons and years. Of Bruestle's expressive landscapes, a critic for the *New York Times* wrote in 1918: "The sharp, full color and well-nourished surfaces of Mr. Bruestle's interpretations of nature give pleasure of a tonic kind."

UNTITLED LANDSCAPE. n.d.
Oil on artist's board, 3 x 4 in.
*Florence Griswold Museum,
Gift of the Estate of
Mary Griswold Steube
1998.7.9*

**UNTITLED LANDSCAPE
WITH BARN.** n.d.
Oil on artist's board, 3 x 4 in.
*Florence Griswold Museum,
Gift of the Estate of
Mary Griswold Steube
1998.7.13*

**UNTITLED LANDSCAPE
WITH FARM.** 1935.
Oil on artist's board, 3 x 4 in.
*Florence Griswold Museum,
Gift of the Estate of
Mary Griswold Steube
1998.7.14*

MARY CASSATT (1844–1926)

DENISE AT HER DRESSING TABLE. ca. 1908–1909. Oil on canvas, 32⅞ x 27⅛ in.
*Metropolitan Museum of Art, NY, U.S.A., Bequest of Gioconda King, 2004 (2005.129).
Image copyright © The Metropolitan Museum of Art. Image source: Art Resource, NY*

In this intimate portrayal of Denise—apparently a professional model that Cassatt painted several times—as she inspects her coiffure, the artist emphasizes the broad theme of female vanity by focusing on the play of reflections. Both the large mahogany framed mirror and the hand mirror backed in green moiré appear in several other canvases by Cassatt, who is best known for her images of women and children in domestic interiors. Though this painting dates from near the end of her career (her failing eyesight forced her to stop painting altogether in 1914), the unfinished section at the upper right demonstrates the rapid brushwork that she first adopted in her earliest experiments with the Impressionists in Paris in the late 1870s.

WILLIAM CHADWICK (1879–1962)

IRISES. n.d. Oil on canvas, 25 x 30 in.
Florence Griswold Museum, Gift of Elizabeth Chadwick O'Connell 1975.7.5

Chadwick painted this luxuriant landscape in the coastal town of Old Lyme, Connecticut, where a lively art colony had emerged in the summer of 1900 centered around the boarding house of Florence Griswold. The colony soon became a bastion of American Impressionism, attracting well established artists such Childe Hassam and Willard Metcalf, as well as younger painters such as Chadwick, who had studied figure painting under Joseph DeCamp in Boston but began to experiment with landscape painting in Old Lyme. Eventually he developed the distinctive Impressionist style seen in this canvas, which is marked by a colorful palette, broad brushstrokes, and a dynamic composition that incorporates strong diagonals. The luxuriant cluster of irises appear to grow wildly, reflecting the "cottage garden" style much in favor at the turn of the twentieth century in the United States.

UNTITLED LANDSCAPE. n.d. Oil on artist's board, 14¼ x 18¼ in.
Florence Griswold Museum, Gift of Elizabeth Chadwick O'Connell, 1977.3.14

Chadwick was a central figure in the art colony at Old Lyme, Connecticut, which he first visited in 1902 with his friends from the Art Students League in New York. He spent several subsequent summers at the boarding house operated by Florence Griswold, where he gradually absorbed the influences of the colony's older painters, particularly Willard Metcalf. Incorporating elements from both the Old Lyme School and his instructor at the Art Students League, the Boston School painter Joseph DeCamp, Chadwick developed his own conservative impressionistic style marked by delicate and subtle tones. In 1915 Chadwick and his wife purchased their own house on Johnny Cake Hill in Old Lyme, and for the next forty years he carried on the Impressionist tradition of painting the seasonal changes in the surrounding countryside.

WILLIAM MERRITT CHASE (1849–1916)

THE CONNOISSEUR-IN THE STUDIO CORNER. ca. 1885
Oil on canvas, 20⅛ x 24⅛ in. *Arkell Museum at Canajoharie, Gift of Bartlett Arkell, 1945*

From 1878 to 1895, Chase worked in the Tenth Street Studio Building in New York's Greenwich Village. Designed by the American architect Richard Morris Hunt and built in 1857, it was the first modern studio building of its type in New York, a welcome addition for artists who had formerly been relegated to small, cold, poorly lit attic rooms above commercial establishments or in boarding houses. Artists from all over the country flocked to the Tenth Street Building to work, talk, teach, exhibit, and sell their creations. For Chase, the studio he occupied also served as a marketing tool, a way for him to proclaim himself as a knowledgeable connoisseur, a voracious collector, and an artist of consequence. The exotic, richly decorated space he created was intended to represent a level of taste, affluence, and European sensibility that would appeal to patrons in Gilded Age New York.

BATH BEACH: A SKETCH (BENSONHURST). ca. 1887
Oil on canvas, 27 x 49¾ in. *Parrish Art Museum, Southampton, NY,
Gift of Mrs. Robert Malcolm Littlejohn, Littlejohn Collection, 1961.4.24*

Between 1886 and 1890 Chase created a series of small paintings of parks and harbors in Brooklyn and New York City that are recognized today as the earliest American landscape paintings in the Impressionist style. This one depicts the seaside walkway along Bensonhurst Drive in the Brooklyn resort of Bath Beach, a popular destination for families escaping the heat of the city. In the 1880s, the road was lined by stylish hotels and yacht clubs, while further inland stood summer villas occupied by middle- and upper-class women and children whose husbands and fathers joined them there on weekends. Chase's painting would have reflected the respectability of the resort, where families could stroll carelessly while enjoying the breeze. The cannon visible on the walkway represents the historic military role of Fort Hamilton, which served as a training center during the American Civil War.

THE POT HUNTER. 1894. Oil on canvas, 16¼ x 24⅛ in.
Parrish Art Museum, Southampton, NY, Purchase Fund and Gift of Mr. Frank Sherer, 1974.5

Chase painted a number of landscapes during the 1890s at Shinnecock, Long Island, the site of the Shinnecock Hills Summer School of Art, where he began teaching in 1891 and which flourished until 1902. It became the most famous school for outdoor work in the United States, the perfect analogue to French art colonies such as Giverny, Grez, and Barbizon. In this canvas, Chase's exploration of bright sunlight, wide open sky, and rich painterly effects convey the pleasure he took in the landscape he had chosen for his summertime work. Many of Chase's Shinnneock landscapes also convey a sense of emptiness and loneliness, some even in spite of human presence. This painting was illustrated as *The Road through the Fields* in George Parsons Lathrop's story "Monda," which included works by several artists and was published in *The Monthly Illustrator* in 1895.

WILL HOWE FOOTE (1874–1965)

LOBSTER TRAPS, CAPE ANN. n.d. Oil on wood panel, 7 x 9 in.
Florence Griswold Museum, Gift of Mrs. Dorothy Clark Archibald 1999.28.2

Cape Ann, Massachusetts, situated just north of Boston and comprising the city of Gloucester and towns of Rockport, Manchester, and Essex, has attracted artists since the eighteenth century. The area also has a rich commercial history as a maritime center and a source of granite for major East Coast building projects. In this painting Will Howe Foote alludes to that commercial maritime history while also capturing the pictur-esque aspects of the seaside towns that have proven so alluring to artists and tourists over the years. Foote studied painting in Chicago, New York, and Paris, and was the youngest of the artists associated with the Old Lyme art colony, which he first visited in 1901 at the age of twenty-seven. Though he spent more than six decades painting there, he was a perfectionist and destroyed any canvas that he didn't consider his best, thus relatively few of his Connecticut landscapes remain.

WILLIAM GLACKENS (1870–1938)

UNDER THE TREES, LUXEMBOURG GARDENS. 1906. Oil on canvas, 19½ x 24¼ in.
Munson-Williams-Proctor Arts Institute, museum purchase, 50.15

Beginning with his first trip to Paris in 1895, Glackens executed a number of compositions of the Luxem-bourg Gardens. This one dates to 1906, when he and his wife, artist Edith Dimock, whom he had wed in 1904, were enjoying a delayed honeymoon in Europe. The festive ambiance of this painting was charac-teristic of Glackens's outlook on life. He was attracted to the gaiety of the modern scene, and preferred to portray life's more pleasant aspects. The work's dark palette is typical of works he painted before 1910 and reflects his interest in the French painter Edouard Manet, who was a key figure in the transition from Realism to Impressionism. Glackens spent a lot of time looking at works by Manet, whose influence can also be seen in the choice of subject matter, the broad painterly treatment of pigment, and roughly suggested figures and details.

BEACH AT NOVA SCOTIA. 1910. Oil on canvas, 18 x 30 in.
Arkell Museum at Canajoharie, museum purchase 1958

Though urban subjects had defined Glackens's early career, beach scenes came to represent an increasingly important theme for him after 1908 and helped to define his growing reputation. He visited the coastal area of Chester, Nova Scotia, in the summer of 1910 and principally devoted himself to bathing and beach scenes, and depictions of piers, harbors, and boats. *Beach at Nova Scotia* is a brilliant example, filled with figures and action—almost like a city scene in terms of activity, but transposed to a more pastoral setting. These summer beach scenes also reflect his transition to a higher-keyed palette, which helps to accentuate the feelings of joy that Glackens appears to have felt about his subject. As one contemporary critic wrote of his beach scenes: "They are true and they are emotional."

LILIAN WESTCOTT HALE (1881–1963)

WOMAN RESTING. ca. 1942. Oil on canvas, 20 x 14 in. *Florence Griswold Museum,*
Gift of The Hartford Steam Boiler Inspection and Insurance Company, 2002.1.171

A genteel woman in a well-appointed interior was a favorite subject for artists of the Boston School, a group of painters centered around the School of the Museum of Fine Arts in Boston in the late nineteenth and early twentieth centuries. Hale was a key member of the Boston School; she studied under Edmund Tarbell in 1897 and in 1901 married Philip Leslie Hale, who was the school's drawing instructor and a major Boston painter. Influenced by fashionable French styles, including Impressionism and Barbizon, as well as earlier eighteenth-century Classical Realism, members the Boston School were known for producing works that blended sophistication and draftsmanship with mastery of light and dedication to representing the "truth" of the visible world. Hale's paintings frequently include a small oil painting displayed on the wall of a room as well as two nearly identical objects—here, the bedposts.

CHILDE HASSAM (1859–1935)

AT THE QUAI, PONT AVEN. 1897. Oil on canvas, 18⅜ x 21⅞ in. *Arkell Hall Foundation*

Situated on the Brittany coast in France, the village of Pont-Aven was a well-known artist's colony frequented by both French and American artists who found irresistible subject matter in the area's quaint stone buildings and picturesque peasants attired in traditional Breton costume. Hassam spent the summer and autumn of 1897 in Pont Aven, where he painted more than a dozen canvases, many of which were enlivened by these timeless figures. This was unusual subject matter for a painter who around this time generally favored modern urban subjects, reflecting the charm these small European villages held for even the most forward-thinking artists.

PROVINCETOWN. 1900. Oil on canvas, 24⅛ x 22⅛ in.
Arkell Museum at Canajoharie, Gift of Bartlett Arkell, 1929

By the 1890s, Provincetown, at the tip of Cape Cod, Massachusetts, was a booming fishing town as well as summer tourist destination popular with artists and writers, who were drawn to its rusticity and small-town feel. Hassam spent the summer of 1900 painting there. In this view of the local scenery, his decision to emphasize the church, its steeple towering over the village and harbor, can certainly be seen as a reflection of the Puritan values he espoused over the course of his career. Also noteworthy are the ships he chose to paint in Provincetown Harbor, which include sailing pleasure craft rather than working schooners or steam-boats. These aesthetic choices reflect both his own and his clients' desire to find pre-industrial charm in New England villages they visited.

AMERICAN ELM. 1905 (or 1903?)
Oil on canvas, 20⅛ x 14⅛ in. *Arkell Hall Foundation*

During his long career Hassam created numerous paintings and etchings that focused on trees in summer landscapes. Though they seem uncomplicated at first glance, his paintings such as *American Elm* not only document the evolution of his Impressionist style, but they can also be seen as reflections of his lifelong interest in American heritage. The art historian Elizabeth Broun has written that Hassam portrayed elms and hickories as silent guardians of America's "origin myth." For example, the American Elm, native to the eastern United States, is an extremely hardy tree that can live for several hundred years. Since elm wood had few uses before the twentieth century, trees were often left standing and continued to grow, even as forestland was cleared for farming or settlement. Hassam's choice to focus on the oldest thing standing—here, the Elm tree—reflects his persistent desire to create links to the past.

AMAGANSETT, LONG ISLAND, NEW YORK. 1920. Oil on canvas, 20 x 30 in.
Munson-Williams-Proctor Arts Institute, museum purchase 58.7

In August 1919 Hassam purchased Willow Bend, a shingled house built about 1722, on Egypt Lane in East Hampton, New York. From 1920 to 1934, he worked there every year from mid-May through early November, continuing his longtime pattern of taking his subjects from his immediate surroundings. In this view of the nearby hamlet of Amagansett, Hassam emphasized the area's colonial history, focusing on a quaint cluster of shingled buildings that reflect a sense of conservative Americanness that appealed to the artist. Hassam had always been interested in his own family history, and was proud to be able to trace a direct line from his New England forebears back to their Anglo-Saxon roots. The style of the landscape, with its flattened space and tapestry-like application of paint, especially visible in the grass and trees, illustrates Hassam's embrace of Post-Impressionist developments later in his career.

ERNEST LAWSON (1873–1939)

CONNECTICUT LANDSCAPE. ca. 1902–1904. Oil on canvas, 24 ⅛ x 24 ⅛ in. *Florence Griswold Museum, Gift of The Hartford Steam Boiler Inspection and Insurance Company, 2002.1.84*

As a young man at the Art Students League in New York in the early 1890s, Lawson came under the influence of the popular teacher John Twachtman, who brought him to Connecticut. It was there in Cos Cob with Twachtman and J. Alden Weir that Lawson first painted outdoors and was inspired to study in Paris. A few months into his 1893 sojourn, he decided that "French influence kills if taken in too large a dose ... I will go back to Connecticut and see what I can do." This canvas, painted a decade later, demonstrates his distinctive Impressionist style of fragmented brushstrokes. He placed strongly contrasting dabs of color side by side, challenging the viewer to blend them optically. The effect of shimmering movement, or "crushed jewels" as one critic called it, makes it difficult to distinguish between sparkling water and sunlight glinting off of the grass in the foreground.

WINTER TWILIGHT – BROOKLYN BRIDGE. 1932
Oil on canvas, 17 ½ x 22 ½ in. *Arkell Museum at Canajoharie, Gift of the artist, 1933*

Lawson's work resides somewhere between Impressionism and Realism. He is usually labeled an Impressionist due to his interest in light and atmosphere, his loose brushwork, and his early training at the Art Students League in New York with John Henry Twachtman and at the informal summer school in Cos Cob, Connecticut, with Twachtman and J. Alden Weir. But he has also been linked with the Ashcan School, the Realist art movement that came into prominence in New York in the early twentieth century for portraying the grittier side of city life. Lawson exhibited with both groups, following his own conviction that "what the artist needs more than anything else is to be true to his own individuality." *Winter Twilight-Brooklyn Bridge* is a perfect example of Lawson's ability to capture in one canvas both the reality and the poetry of the urban landscape.

WILLARD LEROY METCALF (1858–1925)

CHILD IN SUNLIGHT. 1915. Oil on canvas, 25 ⅛ x 21 in.
Florence Griswold Museum, Gift of Mrs. Henriette Metcalf, 1979.7.3

Metcalf was a founding member of The Ten American Painters, the group of artists based primarily in Boston and New York who in the 1890s embraced the expressive brushwork, unfinished paint surface, light high-keyed palette, informal compositions, and plein-air technique that are the hallmarks of Impressionist painting. Like many of his contemporaries, Metcalf received early training in Paris, visited the art colonies in the French countryside, and after returning to the United States spent his career traveling constantly in search of inspiring painting sites. *Child in Sunlight* is a portrait of the artist's daughter, Rosalind, painted on a bright summer's day at Pleasure Beach in Waterford, Connecticut, a frequent summer destination for Metcalf and his family.

THE RED MAPLE. 1920. Oil on canvas, 26 x 29 in.
Arkell Hall Foundation

Metcalf painted *The Red Maple* in 1920, near the end of an almost five-decade long career that had begun in Boston in 1874 and exhibited a level of technical mastery that was rare among his contemporaries. Though frequently sidelined by a destructive lifestyle characterized by fitful personal relationships, lavish spending, and heavy drinking, Metcalf's periods of productivity resulted in light-filled, delicately colored Impressionist landscapes that resonated with the critics and the public alike. In his broad, gentle views of New England hills audiences discovered qualities that were reassuringly familiar and truthful to nature in a way that was considered truly American. For a 1920 viewer contemplating this bucolic autumn landscape, it was possible to momentarily escape the harsh realities facing the United States at the time—the paralyzing post-World War I economic recession, the explosion of organized crime in response to Prohibition, and a series of recent race riots, to name just a few.

CLAUDE MONET (FRENCH 1840–1926)

BRIDGE AT DOLCEACQUA. 1884. Oil on canvas, 25⁹⁄₁₆ x 32⅛ in. *Sterling and Francine Clark Art Institute, Williamstown, Massachusetts. Gift of Richard and Edna Salomon, 1985.11*

Revered by the American painters included in this exhibition as one of the founders of Impressionist painting in France, Claude Monet was the most prolific practitioner of the movement's philosophy of painting outdoors and expressing one's perceptions of nature. *Bridge at Dolceacqua* dates to the middle of Monet's career, following his 1883 move to the village of Giverny. This canvas reflects his twin tendencies during this period to travel in search of compelling subject matter and to paint in series; there are two other paintings that depict nearly identical views of the bridge, and another that takes a longer view of Dolceacqua, the small town on the Italian coast just west of the French border. The view here is of the medieval bridge over the river Nervia and the chapel of San Filippo Neri, which he painted from the opposite bank at the foot of the "Borgo Antico," or old town.

EDWARD W. REDFIELD (1869–1965)

SLEIGH BELLS. ca. 1920. Oil on canvas, 28 x 32 in.
Arkell Museum at Canajoharie, Gift of Bartlett Arkell, 1926

Redfield was one of the Pennsylvania Impressionists working around New Hope in the late nineteenth and early twentieth centuries. Best known for the winter landscapes he painted in the plein air tradition, Redfield made no preliminary studies or drawings. Instead he worked straight onto the canvas, rapidly and forcefully wielding brushes heavy with paint. He almost always completed his canvases in one session without any later touch-ups, creating a true sense of immediacy and vitality. The sleighs at the center of this work were a standard mode of winter transportation before the advent of automobiles, which were becoming increasingly popular in the boom years following World War I. By 1920 Ford had already sold more than one million passenger vehicles. Perhaps Redfield was already feeling nostalgic for the cheerful sound of sleigh bells, which he knew would soon be replaced by the immensely less charming din of automobiles.

THEODORE ROBINSON (1852–1896)

AUTUMN SUNLIGHT (IN THE WOODS). 1888. Oil on canvas, 18⅛ x 21¾ in. *Florence Griswold Museum, Gift of The Hartford Steam Boiler Inspection and Insurance Company, 2002.2.114*

The Vermont-born son of a Methodist minister, Robinson spent much of his career in France, where he painted primarily landscapes and female figures influenced by academic styles before embracing Impressionism in 1888 in the small village of Giverny. This is one of the first works he painted there. The peasant woman takes a break from her task of gathering firewood to confront the viewer, yet she is so well integrated into her setting that she has all but merged with the landscape. This symbolic union of women and nature was a common preoccupation of the American Impressionists. Robinson first exhibited this work in 1889 in New York at the annual exhibition of the Society of American Artists, an organization of avant-garde painters and sculptors formed in 1877 in opposition to the more conservative National Academy of Design.

JOSEPHINE IN THE GARDEN (AT THE FOUNTAIN). ca. 1890
Oil on canvas, 32 ¼ x 26 ⅛ in. *Arkell Museum at Canajoharie, Gift of Bartlett Arkell, 1946*

In 1887 Robinson began a six-year period of extended stays in Giverny, the village northwest of Paris where Claude Monet had settled just a few years before. Monet was likely the reason for Robinson's choice— the town's population was under three hundred, and was a long walk from the nearest train station. While Robinson was one of several Americans who flocked there, he was unique among his compatriots in befriending the reclusive French master. In this painting he depicts his model Josephine in Monet's famed garden. The painting is representative of the style and subject matter of his Giverny canvases, which many consider his finest works. Not only did he adopt techniques of the Impressionist movement, but, like Monet, he became increasingly attuned to the subtle changes in light and color at different moments through the day.

ALLEN TUCKER (1866–1939)

ICE HARVESTING. 1910. Oil on canvas, 20 x 30 in. *Fenimore Art Museum, Gift of Allen Tucker Memorial. Photograph by Richard Walker*

For Tucker, as for many of his fellow American Impressionists working in a period of great progress and change, nostalgia for a simpler way of life was a popular theme. Harvesting ice was a major industry in nineteenth-century New England. Frederick Tudor created the first natural ice business in the United States in 1805, harvesting ice on a pond in Lynn, Massachusetts, that was stored in huge ice houses to allow for year round distribution to destinations, including the West Indies, Calcutta, China, and Europe. Specialized tools such as plows and saws increased efficiency, and commercial ice harvesting boomed across New England. But when Tucker painted this canvas in 1910, natural ice harvesting was in decline. The development of artificial ice manufacturing in the mid-nineteenth century made it possible for ice to be produced year round in factories, and the subsequent invention and popularization of the electric refrigerator in the early twentieth century enabled people to make their own ice at home.

JOHN HENRY TWACHTMAN (1853–1902)

A BREEZY DAY. ca. 1885–1900. Oil on canvas, 20 x 16 in.
Arkell Museum at Canajoharie, Gift of Bartlett Arkell, 1928

Probably executed shortly after his return to the United States after two years painting in Paris and the French countryside, this work reflects a turning point in Twachtman's career: the heavy brushwork and dark, muted tonality he had adopted during his earliest European training in the 1870s in Munich are gone, replaced by a lighter palette and more poetic approach to the landscape that anticipates his fully developed Impressionist style. This painting's spare, elegant design, flattened perspective, high horizon, and vertical orientation echoed by the slender trees also reveal Twachtman's indebtedness to Japanese woodcut prints. The appreciation that many French and American Impressionists felt for Japanese aesthetics is well documented, and it is known that Twachtman and Claude Monet were among those who collected wood-block prints. The road winding into the distance appears in several of Twachtman's paintings of this period.

GLOUCESTER HARBOR. ca. 1900. Oil on canvas, 25 x 25 in.
Arkell Museum at Canajoharie, Gift of Bartlett Arkell, 1939

When Twachtman was painting in Gloucester, the Massachusetts town was the site of a significant ship-building and fishing center that had experienced an influx of Portuguese and Italian immigrant laborers. Yet Twachtman chose to romanticize the seaport, creating a delicately lacy, atmospheric scene. The foreground of trees and foliage, and high vantage point, suggest a rural scene of hills rolling down to the shore. The delicate pier angles into the harbor of placid blue water punctuated by gleaming white sails. The distant shore is equally verdant. While Twachtman was certainly experimenting with avant-garde aesthetic strategies, he was ignoring many realities of turn-of-the-century experience. There is little evidence of laborers or industry—the fish canneries, steam-powered ships, power lines, trolley cars and tracks, and other realities that drove the modern life in the town—but much to suggest why artists and tourists found the area so appealing.

J. ALDEN WEIR (1852–1919)

SUMMER LANDSCAPE, CONNECTICUT. n.d. Oil on canvas, 20⅛ x 24⅛ in.
Arkell Museum at Canajoharie, Gift of Bartlett Arkell, 1945

A versatile painter of landscape, still-life, and figure subjects, Weir was one of the most influential proponents of Impressionist painting in the United States. He began exploring modern French styles during an 1873 to 1877 sojourn in Europe. Back in New York, he was in the vanguard of the group of painters who transformed American art about 1880. He also began a long career as a teacher at the Cooper Union and the Art Students League, and, with his friend and colleague John Henry Twachtman, introduced a number of younger artists to plein-air painting at the informal summer art school in Cos Cob, Connecticut. Weir painted his finest Impressionist landscapes in the area surrounding Branchville, Connecticut, where he purchased an expansive farm in 1882. The following year, he acquired another large property in Windham, Connecticut, and for most of his career he divided his time equally each year between New York City and the Connecticut countryside.

GUY WIGGINS (1883–1962)

A FEBRUARY STORM IN NEW YORK. 1919. Oil on pressed board, 12 in. x 9 in.
Florence Griswold Museum, Gift of Adelaide Dana Bagley in memory of Edwin Gates Bagley, 1992.1

Born in Brooklyn, the son of the artist Carleton Wiggins, Guy Wiggins studied painting at New York's National Academy of Design under William Merritt Chase and Robert Henri. Though he is famous for his Impressionist paintings of New York City in winter, capturing the streets and buildings under quieting blankets of snow, he also painted landscapes throughout New England in all seasons. He became the youngest member of the Old Lyme art colony, where he painted alongside his father and Childe Hassam, whose New York scenes seem to have directly inspired the young painter. Like Hassam, Wiggins portrayed the city as a place inhabited by the wealthy, where streets were clean and wide, commercial establishments upscale, and there was a park around every corner. In this painting, the falling snow softens the city's harsh outlines and obscures its details, creating the effect of muting the urban din.

Endnotes

Optimism, Nostalgia, and Tradition: Impressionism in the United States

1. For more on the Durand-Ruel exhibition, see William H. Gerdts, *American Impressionism* (Artabras, New York, 1984), pp. 51–52.

2. "Suburban Sketching Grounds," *Art Amateur* 25 (September 1891), p. 80.

3. For a detailed analysis of the series, see Barbara Dayer Gallati, *William Merritt Chase: Modern American Landscapes, 1860–1890* (Brooklyn Museum of Art in association with Harry N. Abrams, New York, 2000).

4. For Gallatti's discussion of the painting and photographic postcards of Bath Beach and Bensonhurst Drive from the 1880s, see ibid., pp. 104–105, 108.

5. See H. Barbara Weinberg, *Childe Hassam: American Impressionist* (Metropolitan Museum of Art, New York, and Yale University Press, New Haven and London, 2004).

6. Ibid., p. 93.

7. Stephanie L. Herdrich and Megan Holloway, "Chronology," in ibid., p. 369.

8. Ibid., p. 186.

9. See *Impressionist Giverny: A Colony of Artists, 1885–1915*, ed. Katherine M. Bourguignon (Musée d'Art Américain Giverny/Terra Foundation for American Art and University of Chicago Press, 2007).

10. The details of how and when Robinson met Monet are unclear, but it likely occurred about 1888. See Sona Johnson, *In Monet's Light: Theodore Robinson at Giverny* (Philip Wilson Publishers, London, 2004).

11. Theodore Robinson, "Claude Monet," *Century*, n.s. 22 (September 1982), p. 699.

12. Susan G. Larkin, *The Cos Cob Art Colony: Impressionists on the Connecticut Shore* (National Academy of Design, New York, and Yale University Press, New Haven and London, 2001), p. 1.

13. H. Barbara Weinberg, Doreen Bolger, and David Park Curry, *American Impressionism and Realism: The Painting of Modern Life, 1885–1915* (Metropolitan Museum of Art, New York, distributed by Harry N. Abrams, Inc., New York, 1994), p. 131.

14. Thomas D. Murphy, *New England Highways and Byways from a Motorcar; Sunrise Highways* (L.C. Page and Company, Boston, 1924), p. 279, quoted in Susan G. Larkin, "Hassam in New England," in Weinberg, *Childe Hassam: American Impressionist*, p. 155.

15. "The Lyme Art Show," *Hartford Daily Courant*, September 2, 1902, quoted in Larkin, "Hassam in New England," p. 155.

16. For more on the Gallery-on-the-Moors, including photographs of the interior and exterior, see Larkin, "Hassam in New England," p. 169.

17. *[New York] Sun*, March 19, 1916, section V, p. 8.

Arkell's Most Revealing Light: American Impressionist Paintings from MacBeth Gallery to Canajoharie

1. Tonalism was not used to describe this group of artists until the 1970s. The artists, however, were seen as sharing a distinct "tonal" style and their paintings were marketed to homeowners as part of home decoration. An article in *House & Garden* in 1919 entitled "How to Select Both Old and Modern Types for a Room" used the term *Tonal Masters* to include "George Inness (in his middle and last periods), Homer D. Martin and Alexander Wyant... .and ... Henry Ward Ranger, who perhaps was the closest follower of the Barbizon ideas of any American painter." All of the artists mentioned were in Arkell's personal collection. The Inness paintings added to the Canajoharie Library were not the later Tonalist paintings; they were from his earlier period with landscape views that reminded Arkell of the Mohawk Valley.

2. See E. P. Richardson, *The Role of Macbeth Gallery* (New York City: The American Federation of Arts, 1962) for a history of Macbeth Gallery.

3. *First Exhibition since 1895: Theodore Robinson 1852–1896*, April 19th–May 8th 1943 (New York City: Macbeth Gallery, 1943), includes a number of excerpts of reviews from the first exhibition. These were probably taken from the clippings William Macbeth kept in a scrapbook.

4. Ibid., names Chase as the only buyer at Robinson's first one-man exhibition.

5. *Art Notes* (Macbeth Gallery, April–May 1922), p. 1284.

6. Ibid. p. 1285.

7. Correspondence between Bartlett Arkell and William Macbeth, March–April 1917 (Macbeth Gallery Records, 1838–1968 Archives of American Art, Smithsonian Institution).

8. "Old Bridge at Lyme" is listed as in the Canajoharie Art Gallery on November 27, 1927 in typed letter to Mr. C. Valentine Kirby, Harrisburg, PA (not signed).

9. Lockman's interview with Hassam, February 2, 1927 is quoted in Jay E. Cantor "Beyond Impressionism: Hassam's Twentieth-Century Work," *Childe Hassam Impressionist* (Abbeville Press, 1999), p. 102.

10. For a complete discussion on Hassam's use of American elms in his paintings and the significance and symbolism of the American Elm, see Susan Larkin *The Cos Cob Art Colony: Impressionists on the Connecticut Shore* (Yale University Press, 2001), p. 111.

11. In 1930 a decision was made to exchange *Bridge at Old Lyme*, the first Hassam to enter the Canajoharie Art Gallery, for two works by Charles H. Davis that were already at the Gallery and may have previously been in Bartlett Arkell's private collection. Macbeth wrote to Davis in March 1932 that Arkell had told him that he "wished he had a home in which he could be entirely surrounded by Davis pictures." Another work by Davis, *On the West Wind*, had already entered the Canajoharie collection in January 1929. (Arkell and Macbeth correspondence in Arkell Museum curatorial files and Macbeth Gallery Records, 1838–1968, Archives of American Art, Smithsonian Institution).

12. *American Paintings for Home Decoration* (Macbeth Gallery spring 1928) # 16 Childe Hassam, Brush House, Cos Cob (pastel) 18 x 22.

13. Ibid.

14. See Larkin, *The Cos Cob Art Colony: Impressionists on the Connecticut Shore*, pp.120–123 for a discussion on Hassam and Twachtman's representations of the Brush House.

15. An image of *Breezy Day* was featured as the frontispiece in *The American Magazine Art* (American Federation of the Arts, April 1929) and was listed only as "courtesy of American Art Galleries," with the title *Breezy Day,* but (for no known reason) neither Bartlett Arkell nor Canajoharie Art Gallery are credited as owners. A year earlier the same magazine printed an article about the new museum at Canajoharie with an illustration of the Gallery (fig. 22).

16. Letter to Harrison Morris, Director of Academy of the Fine Arts, from Twachtman, December 2, 1897 (Archives, Pennsylvania Academy of the Fine Arts) who complained that "I do not know the title...and you will have to fill out that part... . a hell of a lot of bother painters have. They not only have to paint the pictures but do a lot

besides." As quoted in Lisa N. Peters *John Twachtman: Painters Painter* (New York City: Spanierman Gallery, 206), p. 28.

17. Letter to Bartlett Arkell from F. E. Barbour, January 10, 1939 (Arkell Museum curatorial files), reporting that Twachtman's *Harbor Scene—Gloucester, Massachusetts* and Tarbell's *Girl Crocheting* were received from William Macbeth, Incorporated without information "as to if they are a further gift from you or what disposition we are to make of them."

18. For a complete discussion on this painting's subject and significance and its exhibition history see Carol Lowrey, "A Girl Crocheting" in *Ten American Painters* (New York: Spanierman Gallery, 1990), pp. 162–165.

19. Letter to Frank Barbour, Canajoharie Library and Art Gallery, from John O'Conner, Jr., Carnegie Institute, Pittsburgh, PA, September 11, 1940.

20. Letter to Frank Barbour from Bartlett Arkell, December 6, 1939 states: "I will send the Chase picture to the Gallery to be retained there. It somehow got to my home and has been there a long time. I know the Gallery will be delighted with this picture, the finest Chase ever painted." Another letter to Frank Barbour from Macbeth Gallery, May 17, 1940, stated that the "real title is 'the Connoisseur' Bart bought it from us in February 1928, one of his early purchases." (Arkell Museum curatorial files). The painting, however, was illustrated and listed as no. 6 with the title *In the Studio in the Macbeth Gallery Sixteenth Annual Exhibition Thirty Paintings by Thirty Artists*, February 28th–March 19th, 1927.

21. For a full discussion on women in Chase's 10th Street Studio and similar paintings by Chase, see Annette Blaugrund, *The Tenth Street Studio Building: Artist-Entrepreneurs from the Hudson River School to the American Impressionists* (Parrish Art Museum, New York, 1997), pp. 118–120.

22. A one page typed annual report from the Arkell Museum Curator, 1988, addresses the removal of Metcalf's *Red Maple* from the Beech-Nut building lobby. Checklists in the 1930s also show this painting in the Library Gallery.

23. *Canajoharie Art Gallery Catalog of the Permanent Collection*, Canajoharie, New York, nd.

24. *Arts Notes* (Macbeth Gallery February 1902), p. 294, calls attention to an exhibition of Redfield's recent works at Macbeth Gallery.

25. J. M. W. Fletcher, *Edward Willis Redfield; An American Impressionist; His paintings and the man Behind the Palette* (Lahaska, PA: JMWF, 1996), p. 179 lists four paintings titled *Sleigh Bells*.

26. Pennsylvania Academy of Fine Arts *Catalog of the exhibition of Landscape Paintings by Edward W. Redfield, April 17 to May 16, 1909.*

27. Bartlett Arkell graduated from Williston Seminary in Easthampton, MA in 1882 and Yale University in 1886.

28. *Art Notes* (Macbeth Gallery November 1930), p. 162.

29. Letter to Frank E. Barbour from Robert McIntyre, January 29, 1942 (Arkell Museum curatorial files), lists three paintings shipped to the Arkell Museum; John Singleton Copley's *Portrait of Dr. Edward Tully*, Winslow Homer's *Shepherdess and Sheep* and Theodore Robinson's *The Brook*.

30. Letter to Frank E. Barbour from Robert McIntyre, May 13, 1943 (Arkell Museum curatorial files).

31. Letter to E. W. Shineman Jr. from Robert McIntyre in Dorset, Vermont, September 26, 1956 (Macbeth Gallery Records, 1838–1968, Archives of American Art, Smithsonian Institution).

32. Letter to Theodore Robinson from Claude Monet, February 26, 1891, printed in Sona Johnson "Monet/Robinson Correspondence," *In Monet's Light: Theodore Robinson at Giverny* (Philip Wilson Publishers, London, 2004), p. 203.

33. A typed page dated December 9, 1958, (Frye Art Museum, Seattle curatorial files) mentions information shared by Mr. Milch and Milch Gallery, *The Wheat Gatherer* "was owned by Theodore Robinson at one time."

34. Quoted from Johnson p. 58.

35. Letter to Thomas A. Warmby Jr. from Robert McIntyre, November 4, 1953 (Macbeth Gallery Records, 1838–1968, Archives of American Art, Smithsonian Institution).

36. Carbon copy of letter to all of the trustees of the Canajoharie Library and Art Gallery from William B. MacKenzie, July 30, 1958 (Arkell Museum curatorial files).

37. The work was in the possession of Mrs. Sadie May when she died, and bequeathed to the Baltimore Museum. It was reportedly de-accessioned from the Baltimore Museum because it had no signature. Knoedler Gallery consigned the Cassatt pastel to Miller Gallery and provided a letter from Martin Jennings to the Canajoharie Curator Ed Lipowicz, September 22, 1958 attesting to the work's authenticity.

38. Letter to William MacKenzie from Elizabeth Grammer, Canajoharie, NY, August 5, 1958 (Arkell Museum curatorial files).

39. Letter to Edward Lipowicz, Curator of the Canajoharie Library and Art Gallery, from Adelyn Breeskin, Smithsonian Institution National Collection of Fine Arts, February 3, 1967 (Arkell Museum curatorial files). An undated note in the files at the National Gallery states that Mathilde Valet served as Mary Cassatt's housekeeper, maid and companion and Adelyn Breeskin reported that Mary Cassatt left her atelier to Mathilde Valet. http://www.nga.gov/collection/gallery/ggc assattptg/ggcassattptg-46482-prov.html
   See Nancy Mowll Mathew *Marry Cassatt: A Life* (Villard Books, 1999), pp. 240–241 for more information and a 1914 photograph of Mathilde Valet (Archives of American Art).

40. A letter from Tom Wharmby, Jr., Curator at the Canajoharie Library, to Robert McIntyre, October 30, 1953, states that the aim is "to build up a first rate collection . . . along the conservative theme begun by Mr. Arkell. ...As I mentioned to you before we want a Glackens and a good one." (Macbeth Gallery Records, 1838–1968 Archives of American Art, Smithsonian Institution).

41. A letter from Ira Glackens to Antoinette Kraushaar, May 14, 1958, states "it was painted there in 1910 when we were spending the summer at the 'Hackmatack Inn.' Incidentally, the small boy at the left, wearing an enormous hat and patting a dog, is myself, aged three." Another letter from Ira Glackens to Caroline Keck dated May 4, 1968, states that "the small boy in the picture with the wide brimmed hat is myself. The work was 'executed' at Chester, Nova Scotia in 1910." (Arkell Museum curatorial files).

American Impressionism Paintings of Light and Life

Lenders to the Exhibition

ARKELL HALL FOUNDATION

ARKELL MUSEUM AT CANAJOHARIE

CLARK ART INSTITUTE

FLORENCE GRISWOLD MUSEUM

THE METROPOLITAN MUSEUM OF ART

MUNSON-WILLIAMS-PROCTOR ARTS INSTITUTE

PARRISH ART MUSEUM

Fig. 14 (*see page 16*). Theodore Robinson (1852–1896)
AUTUMN SUNLIGHT (IN THE WOODS), 1888
Oil on canvas, 18⅛ x 21¾ in. *Florence Griswold Museum, Gift of The Hartford Steam Boiler Inspection and Insurance Company, 2002.2.114*